WILD THINGS

ADULT COLORING BOOK

MADDIE MAYFAIR

© October 2022

All rights reserved.

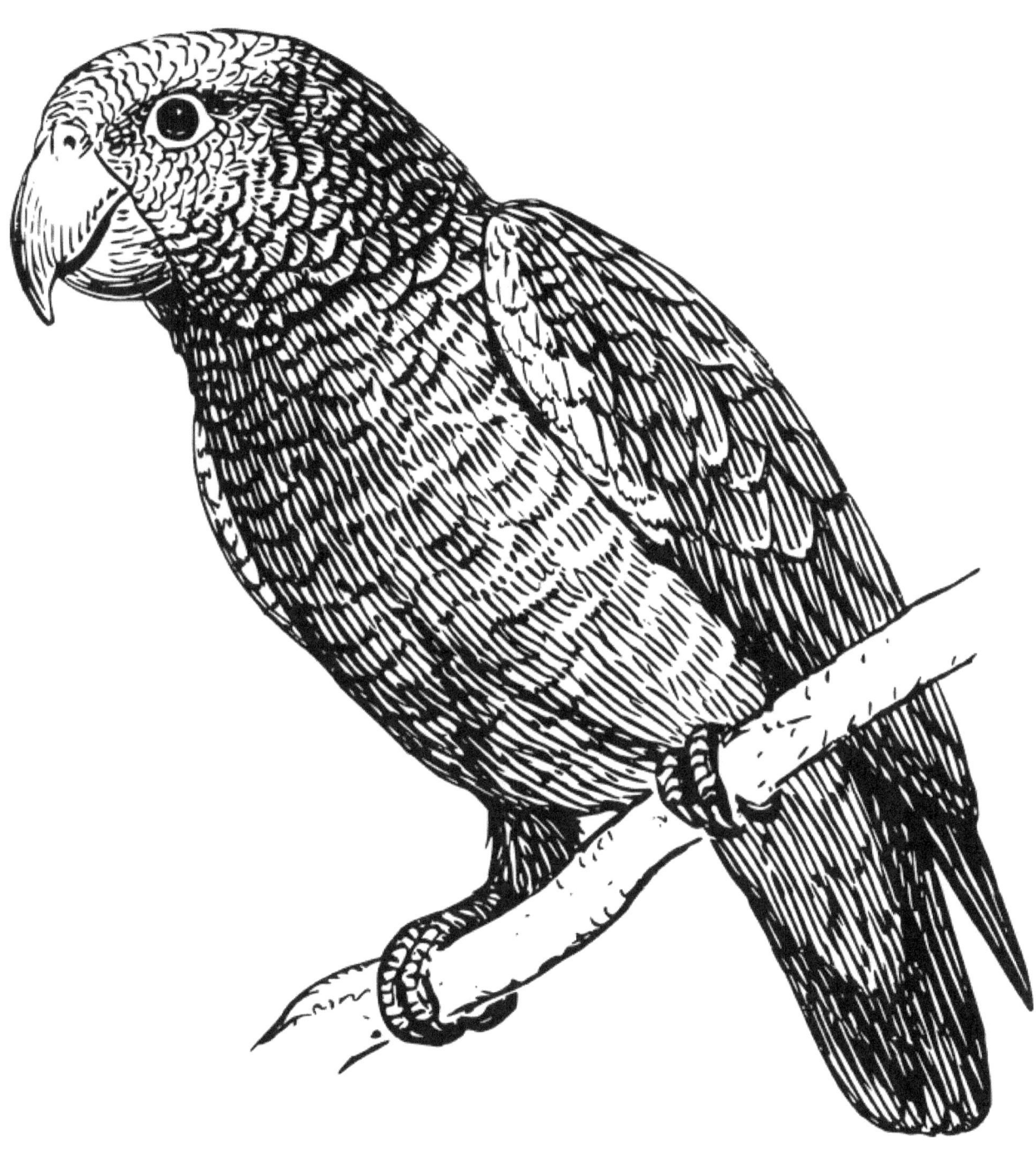

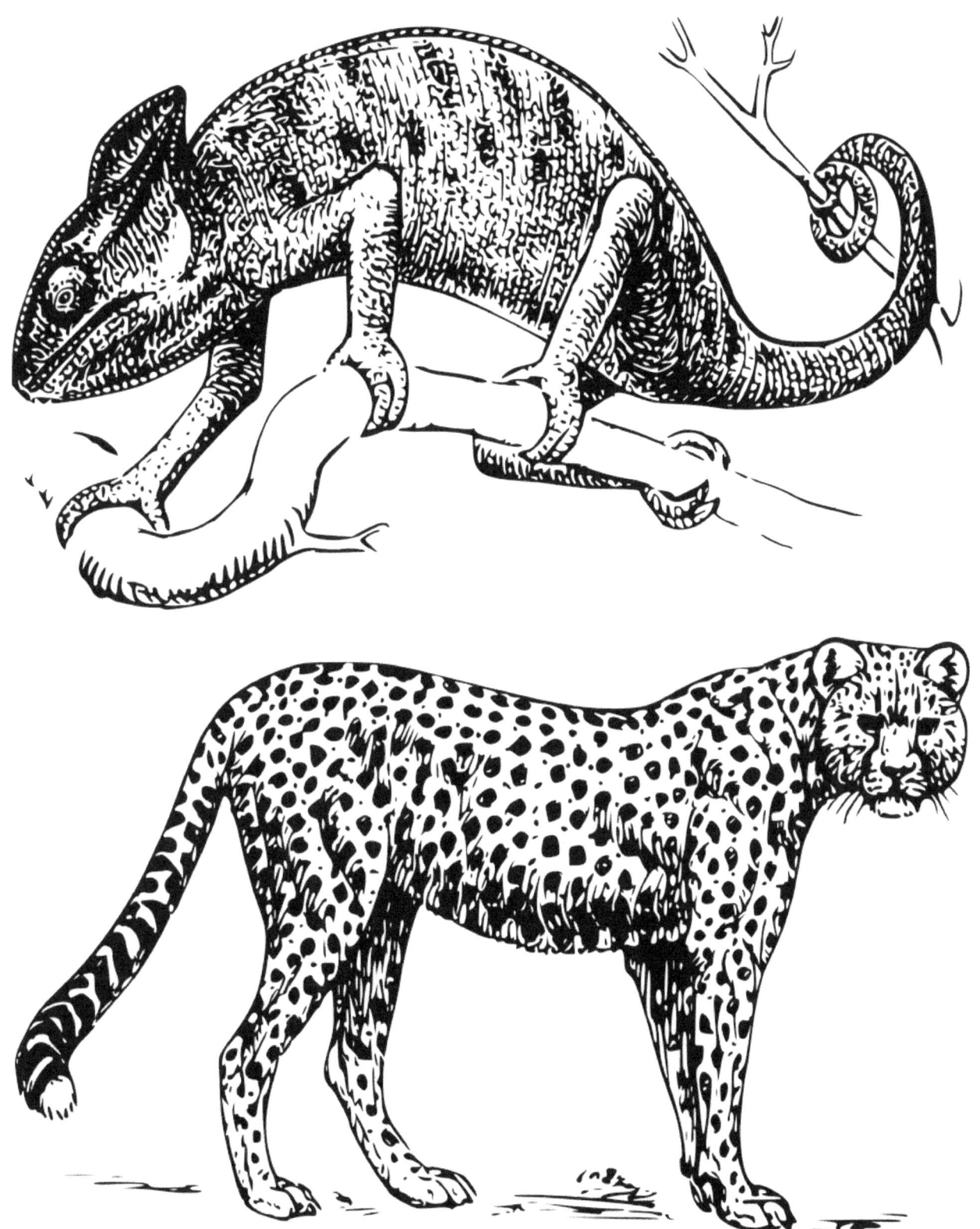

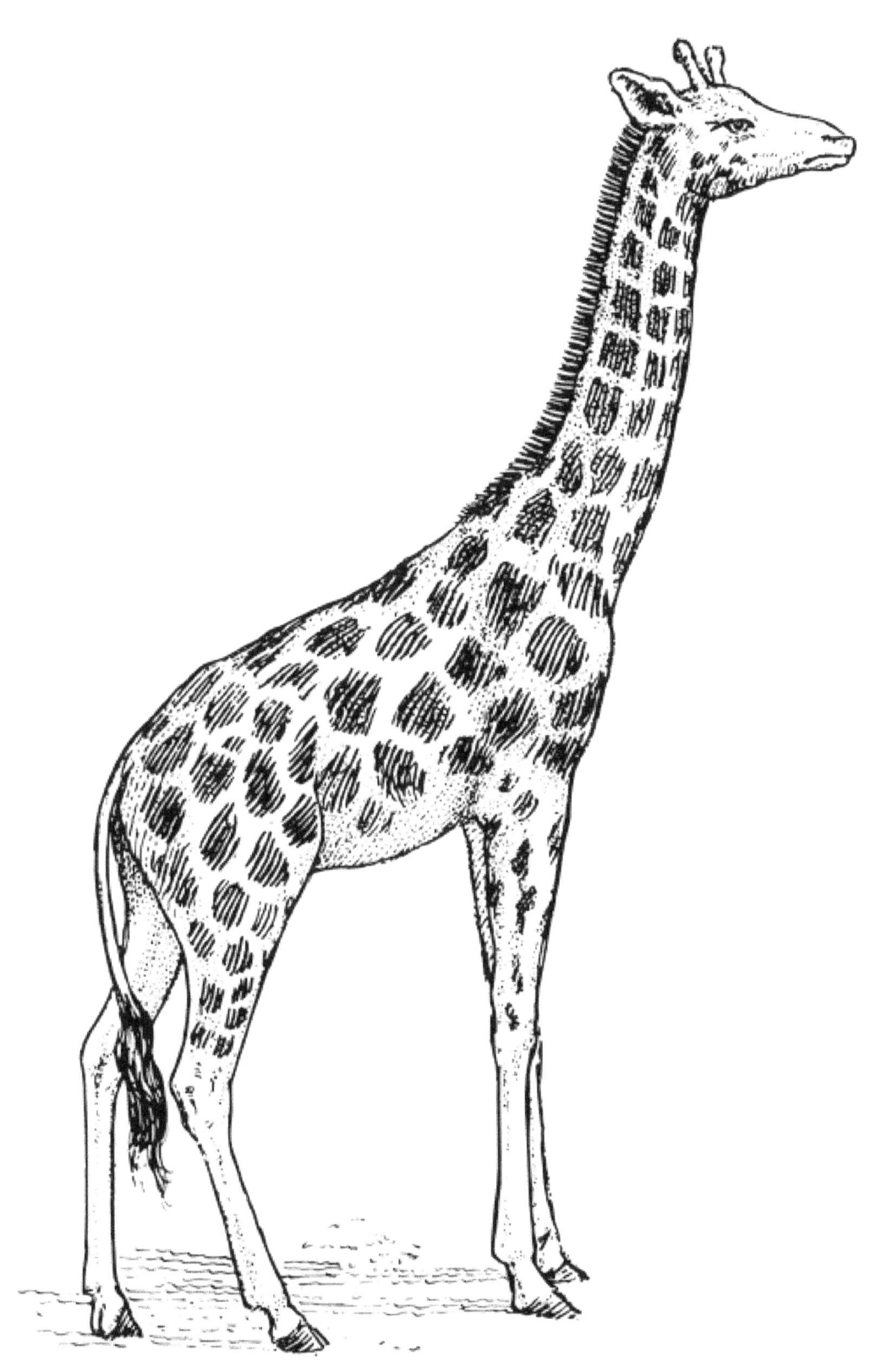

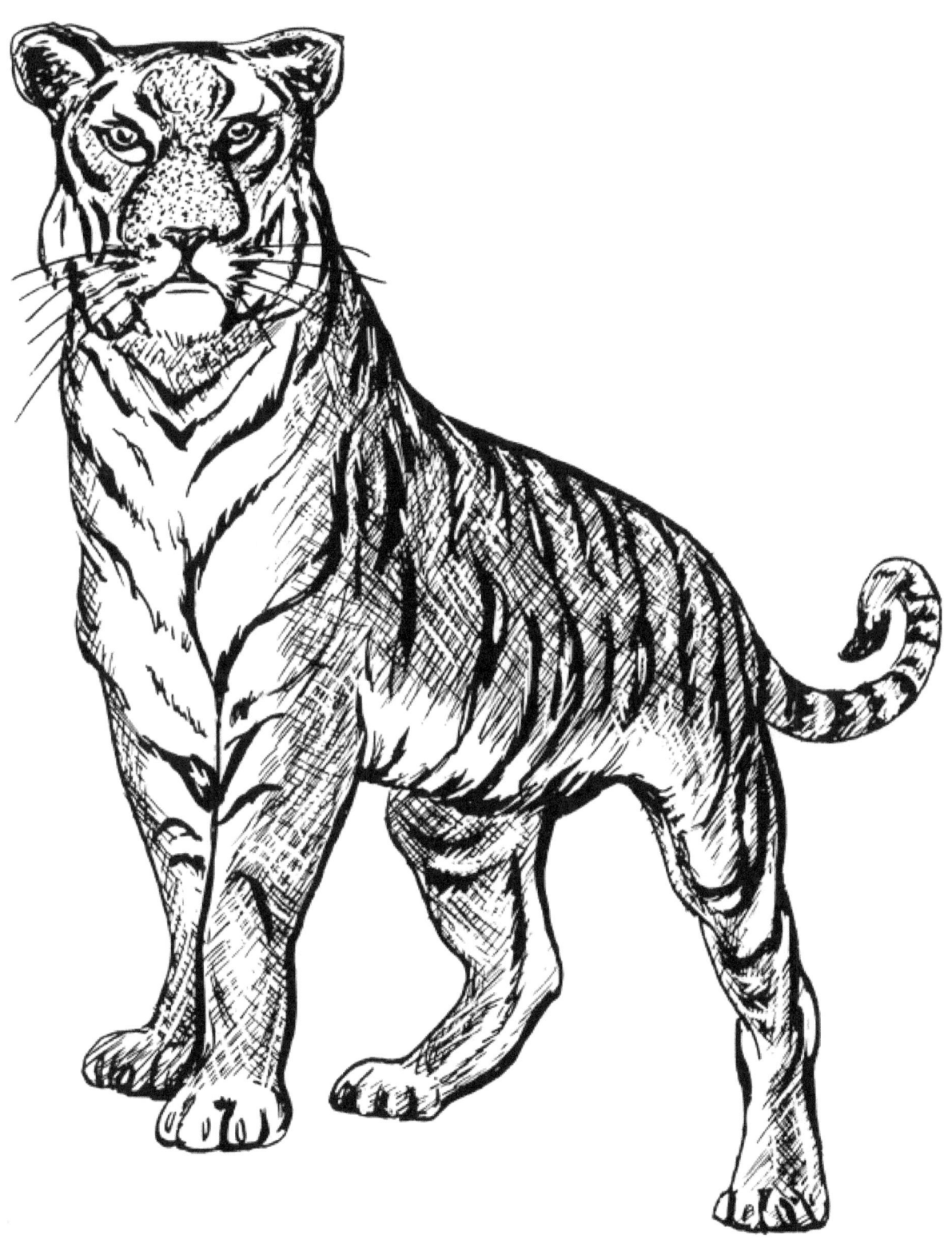

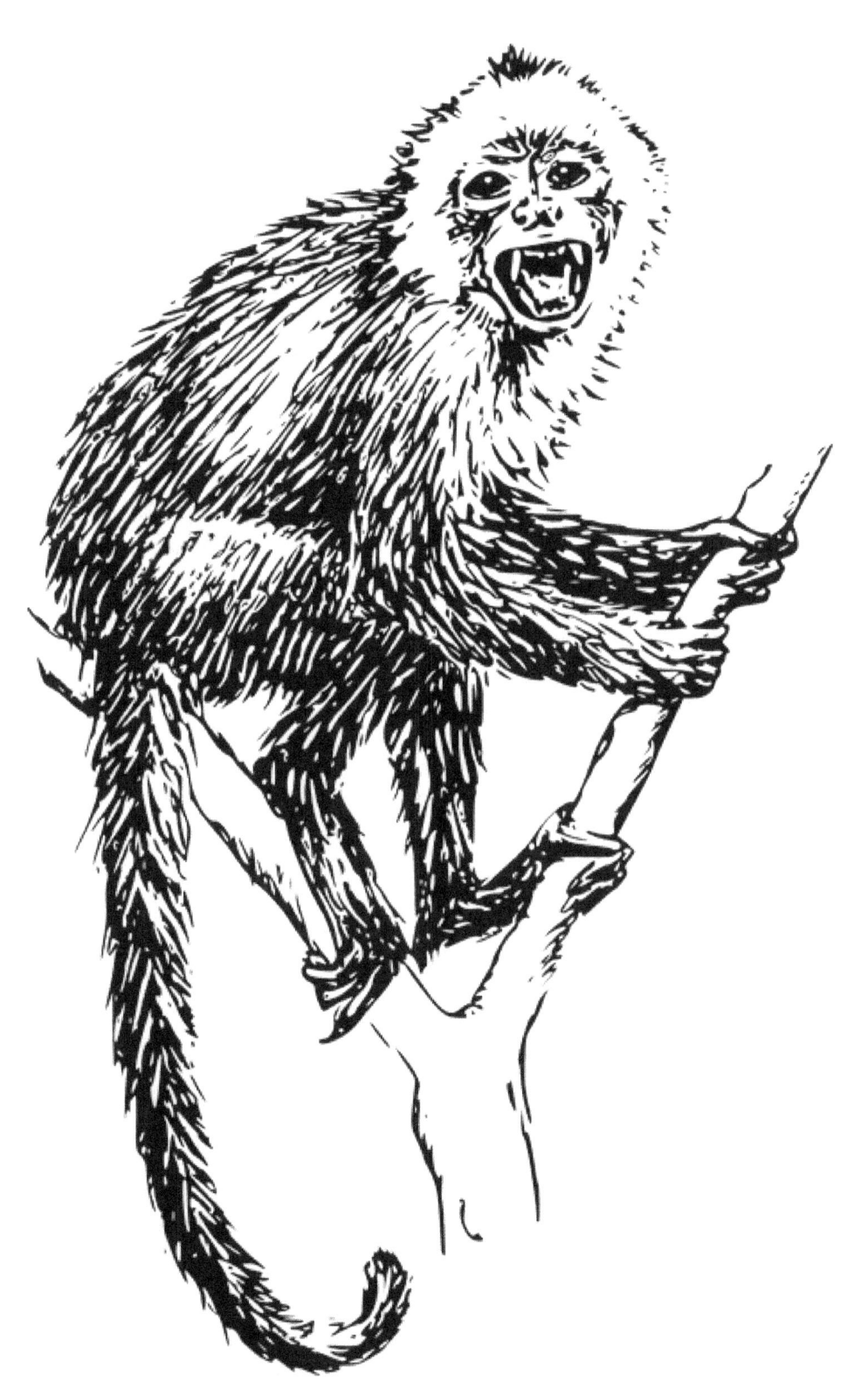

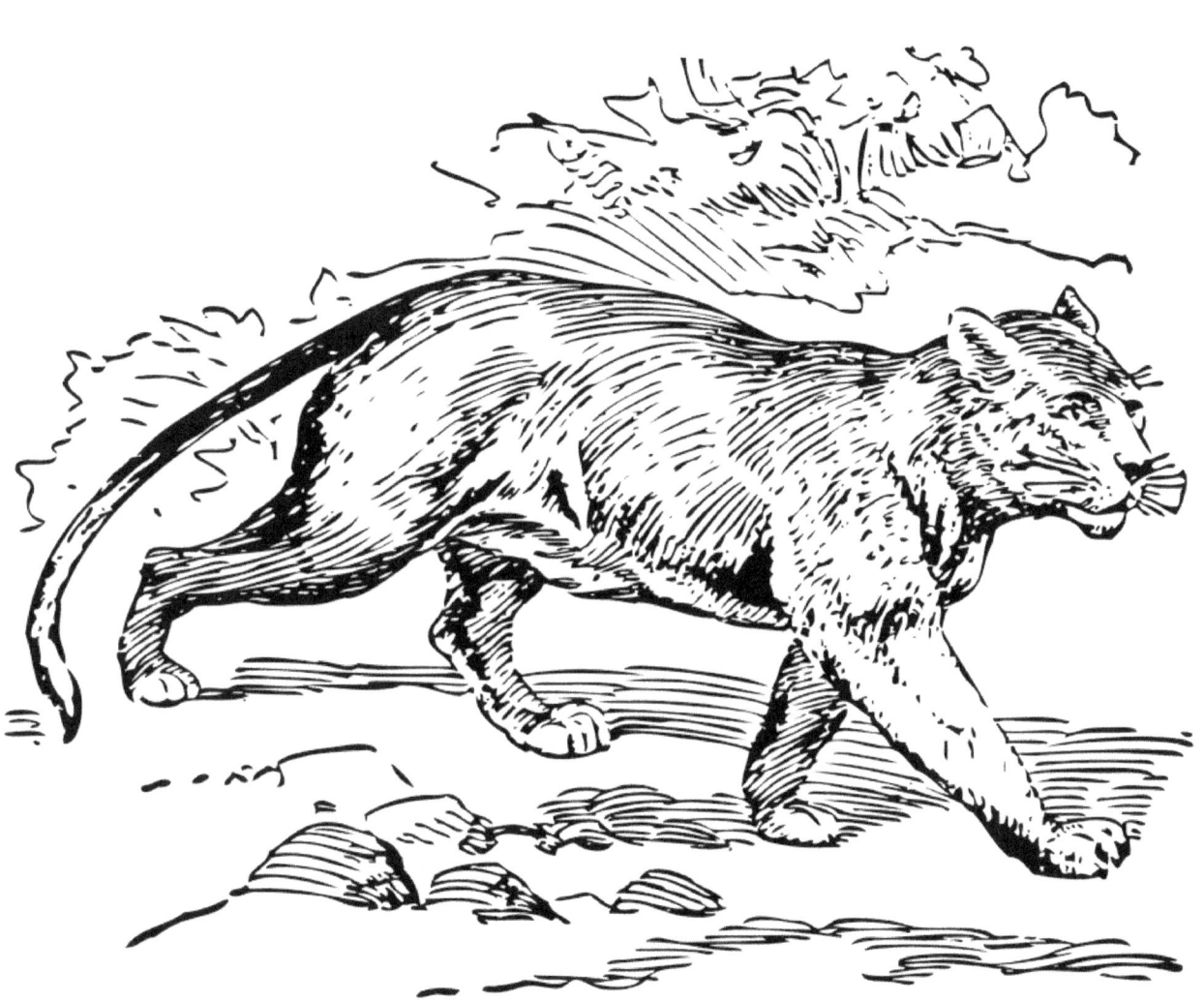

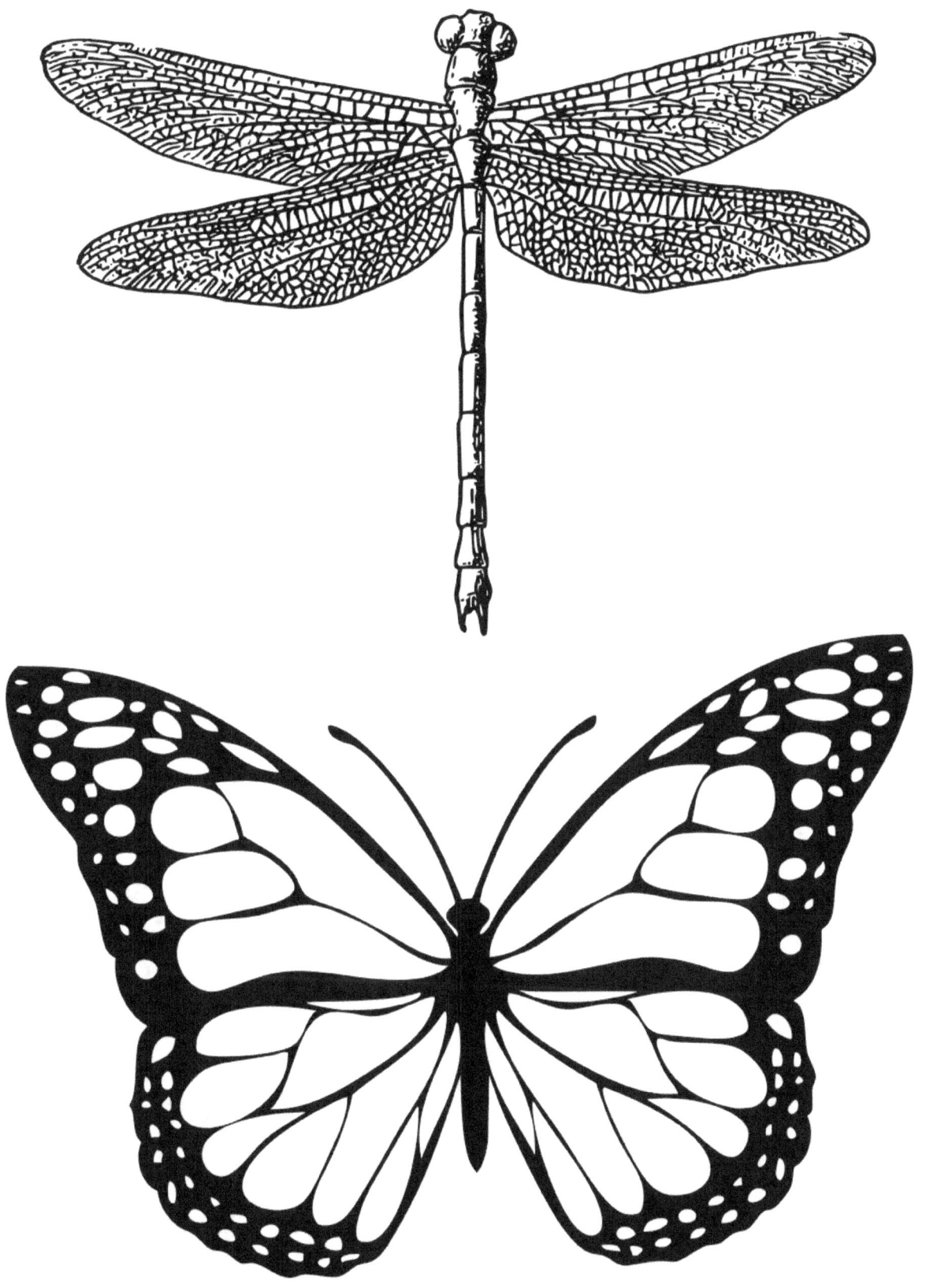

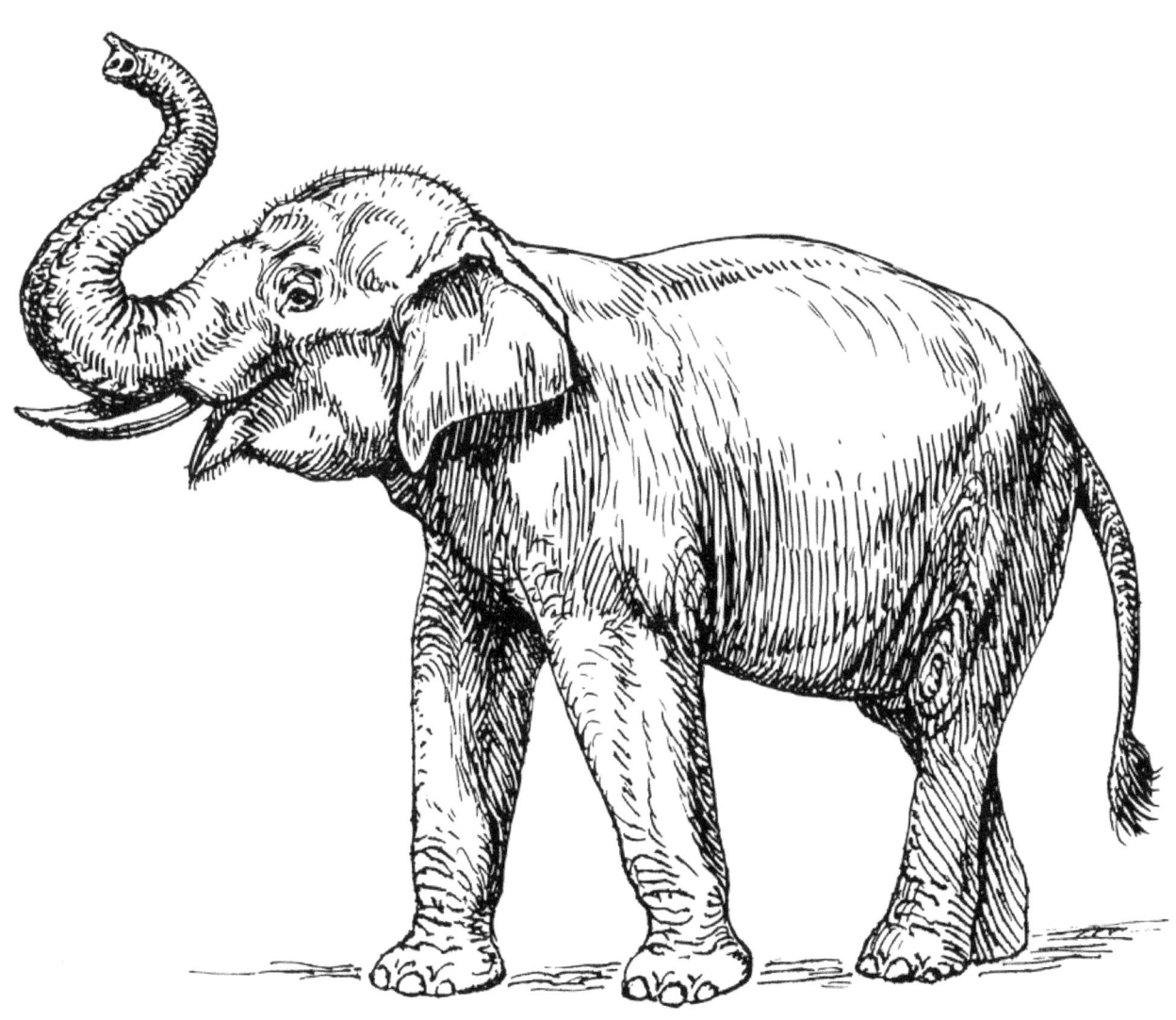

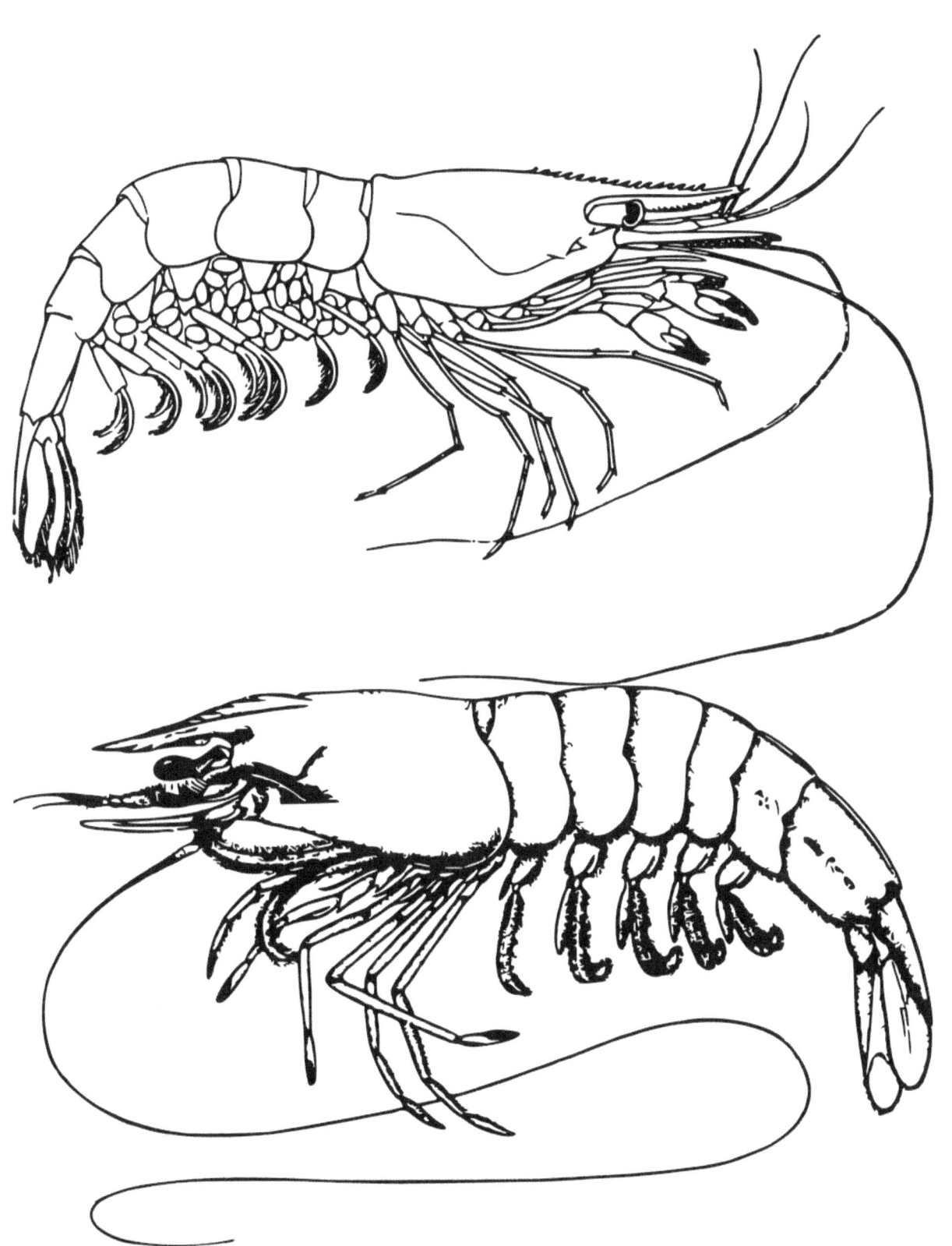

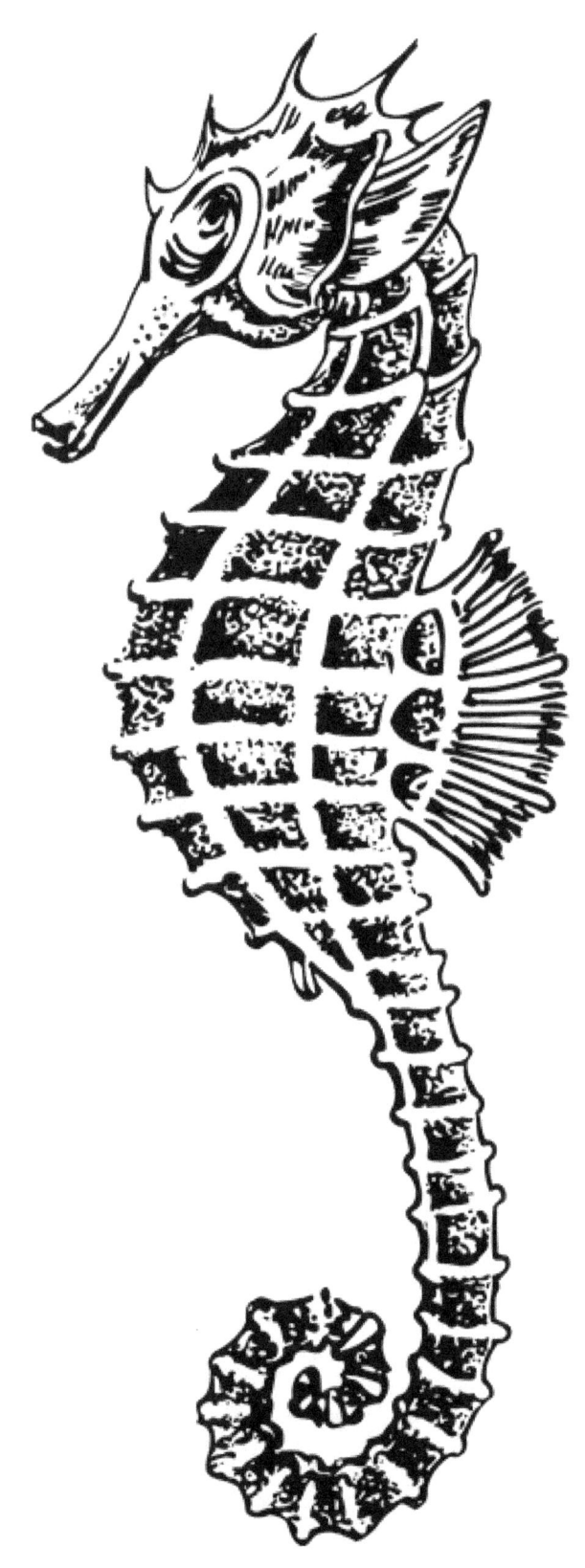

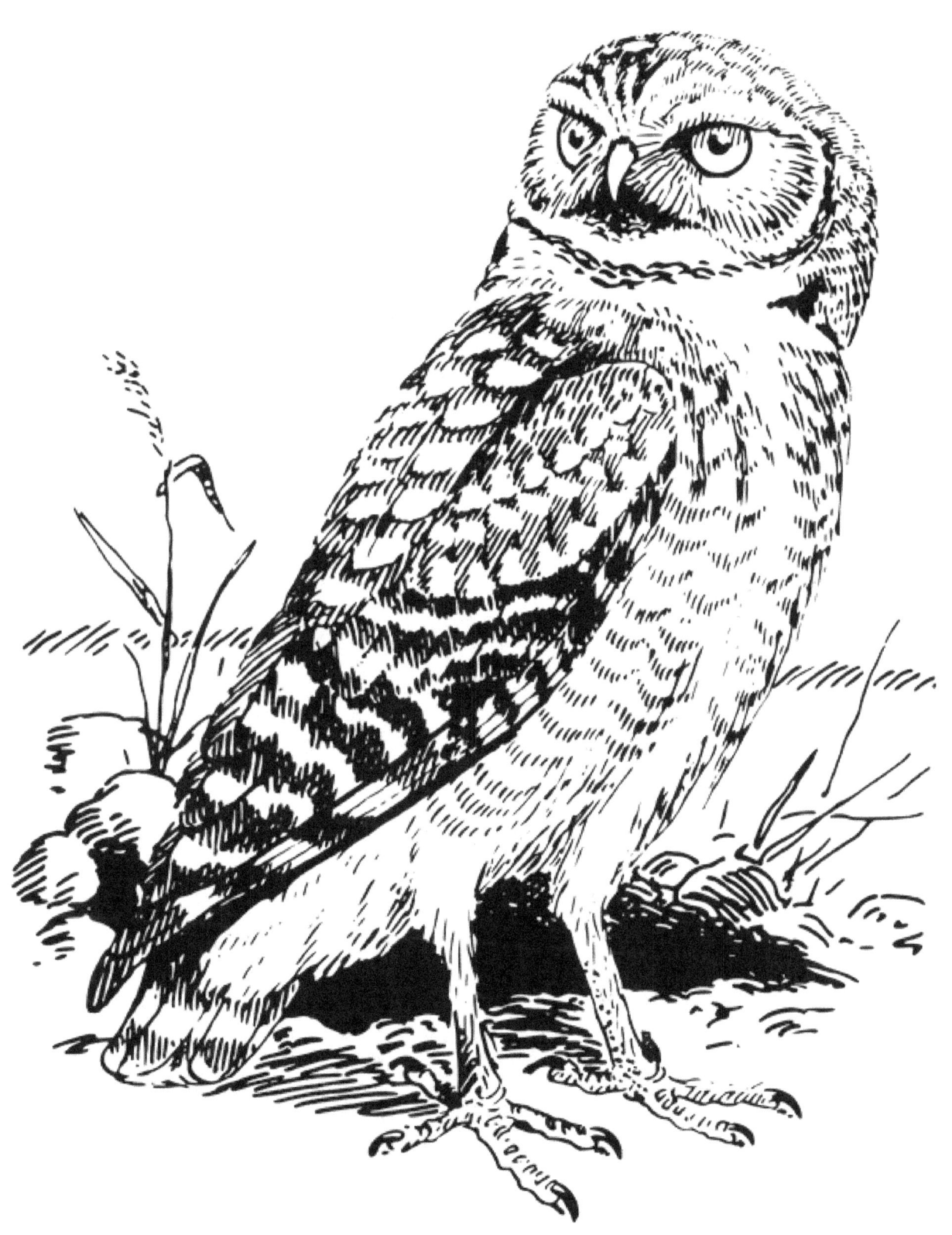

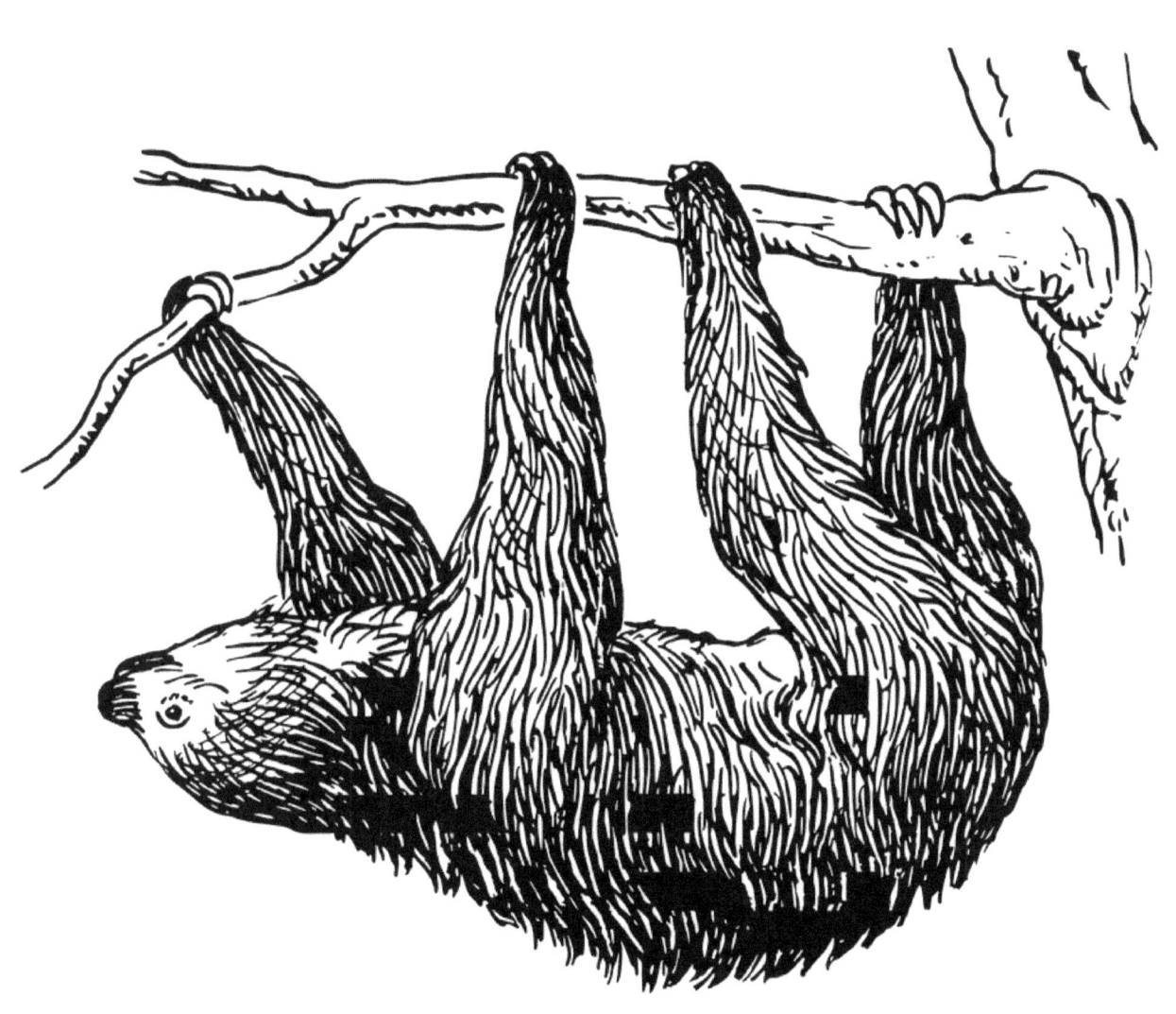

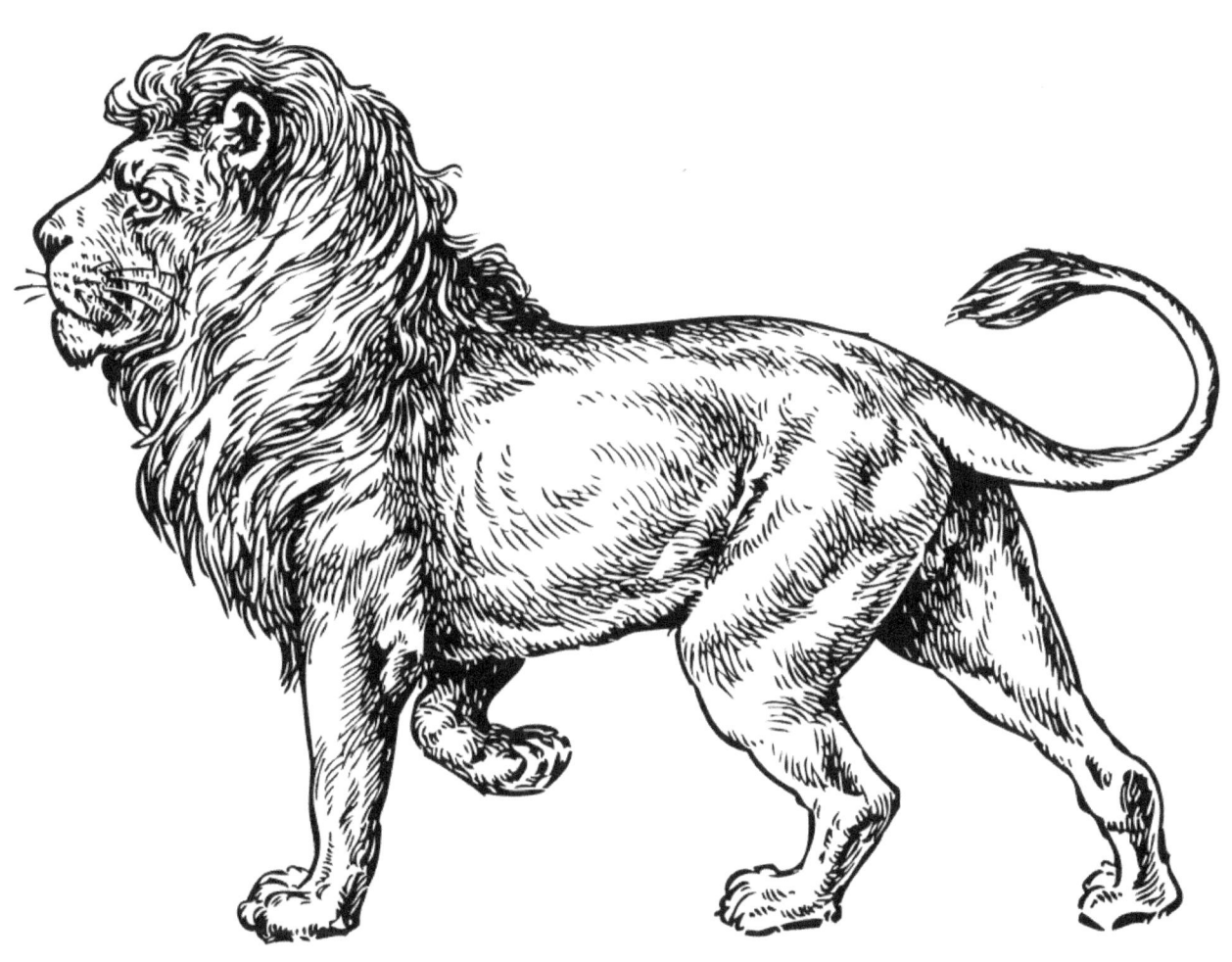

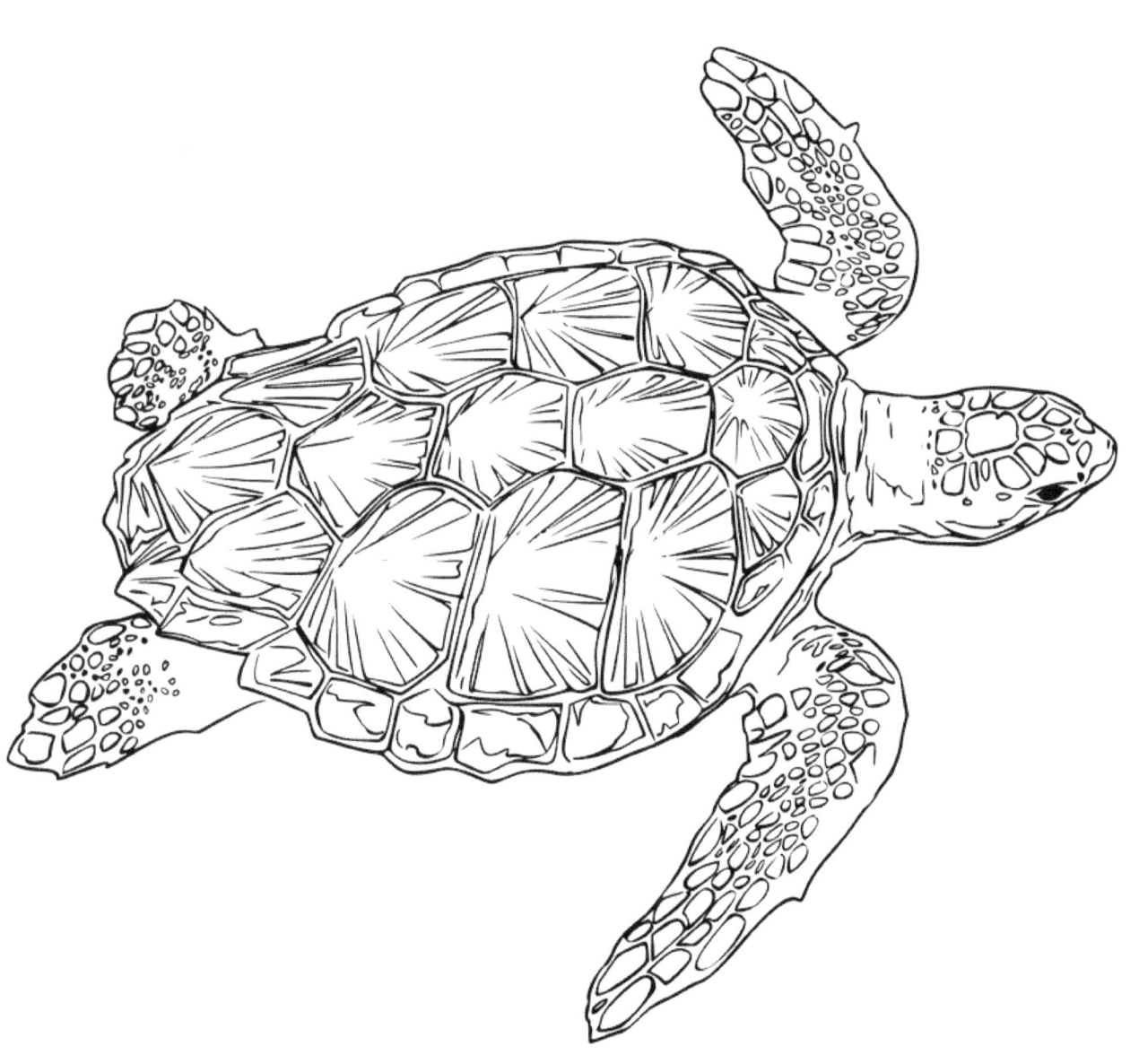

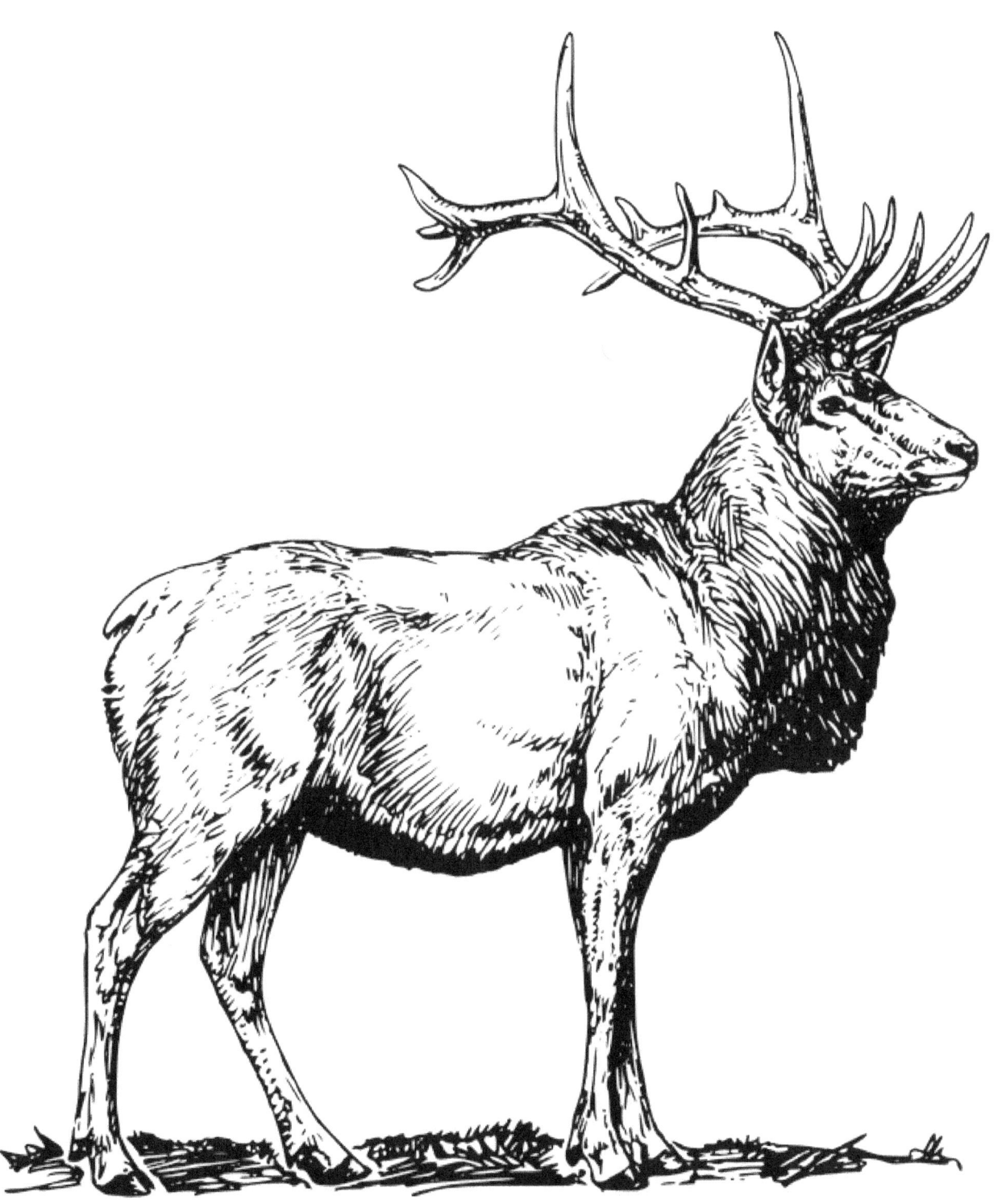

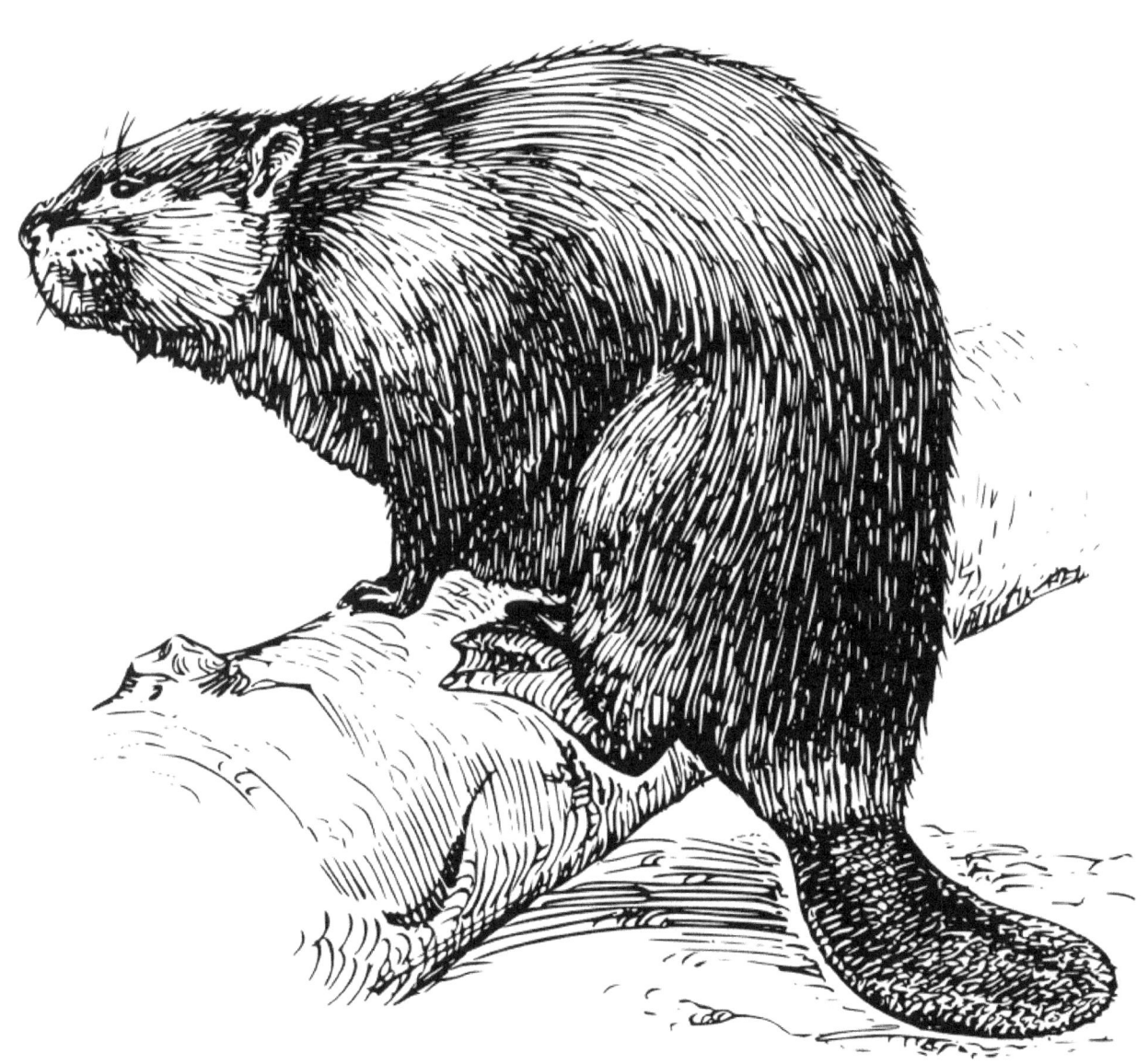

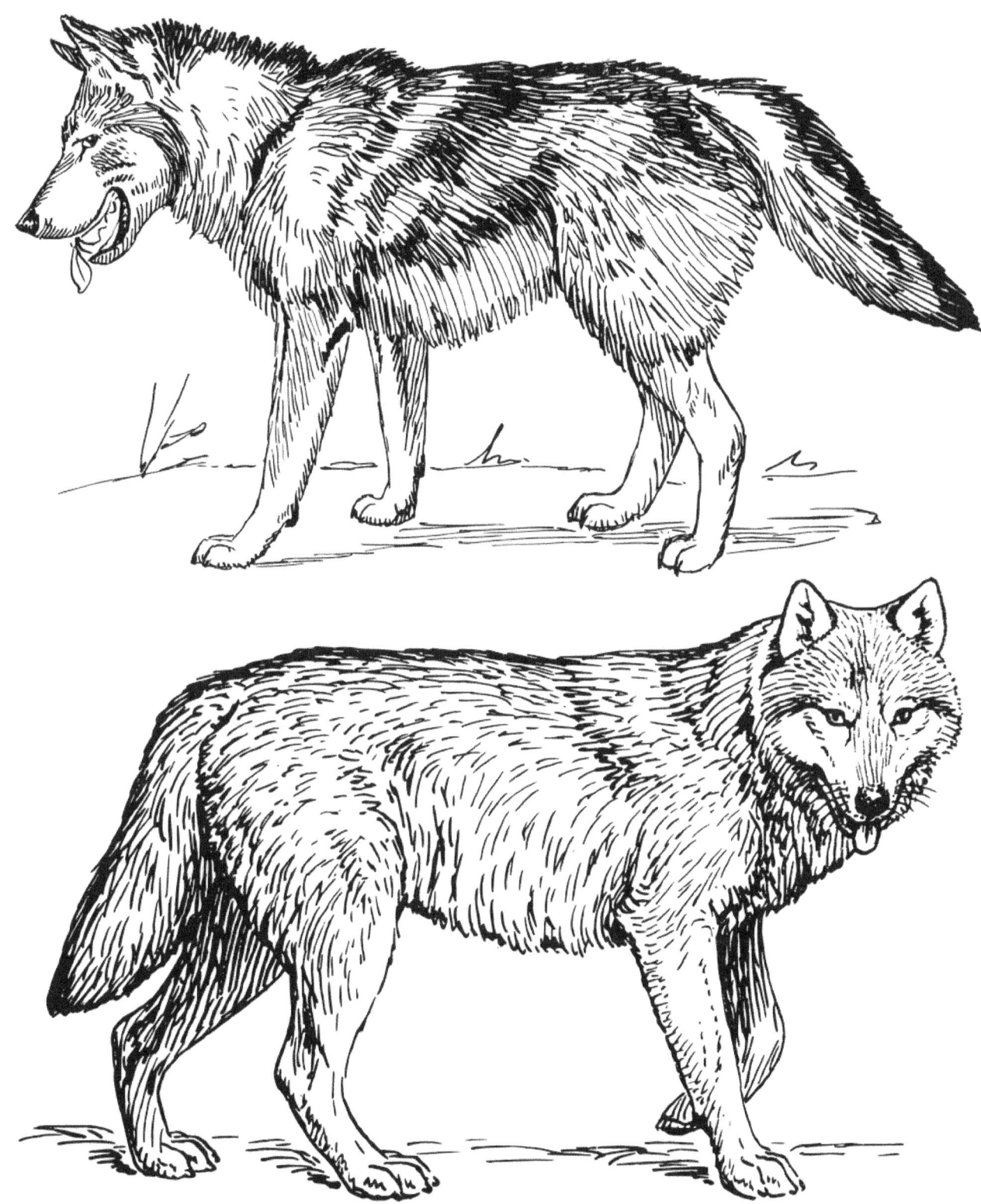

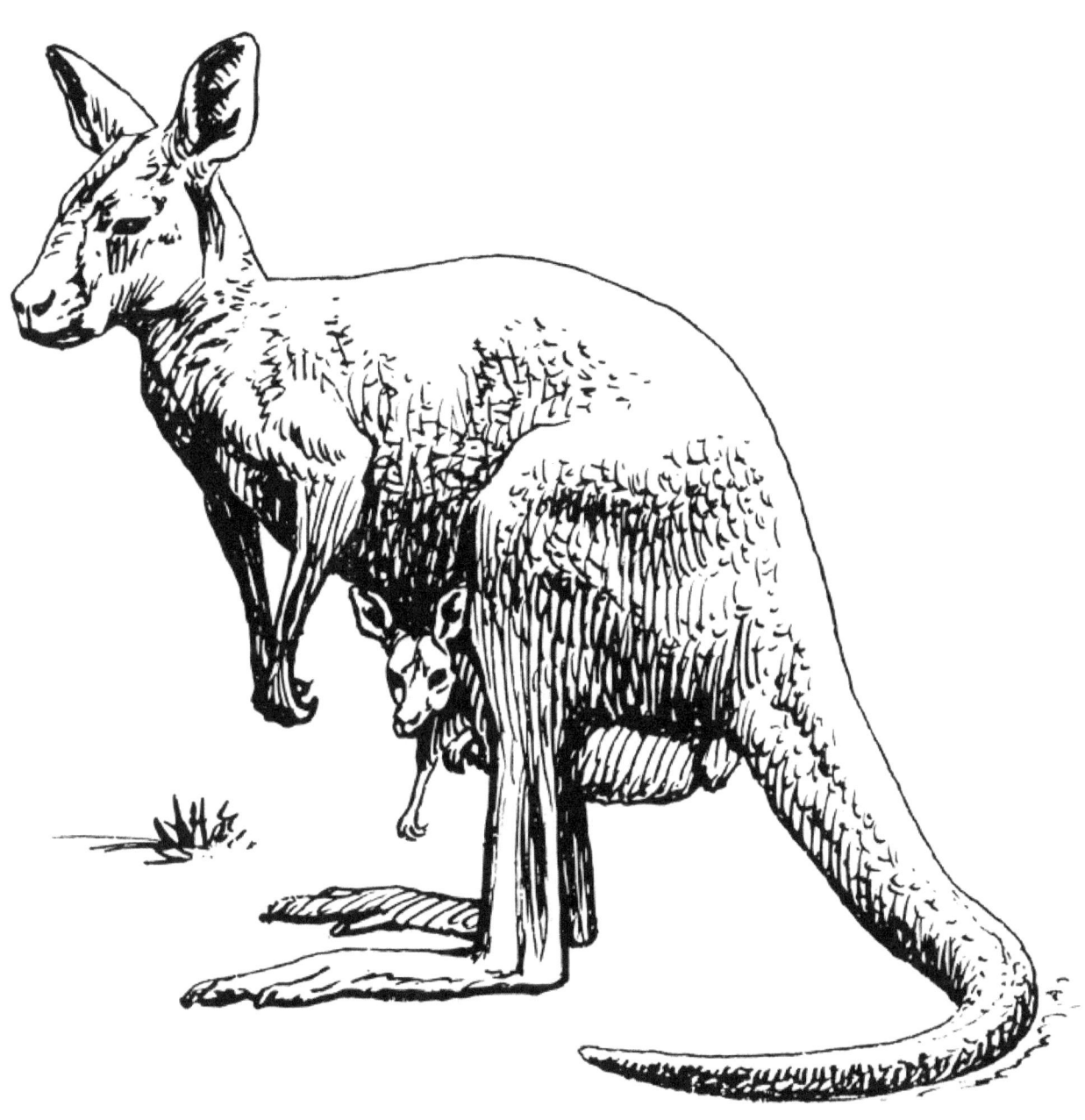

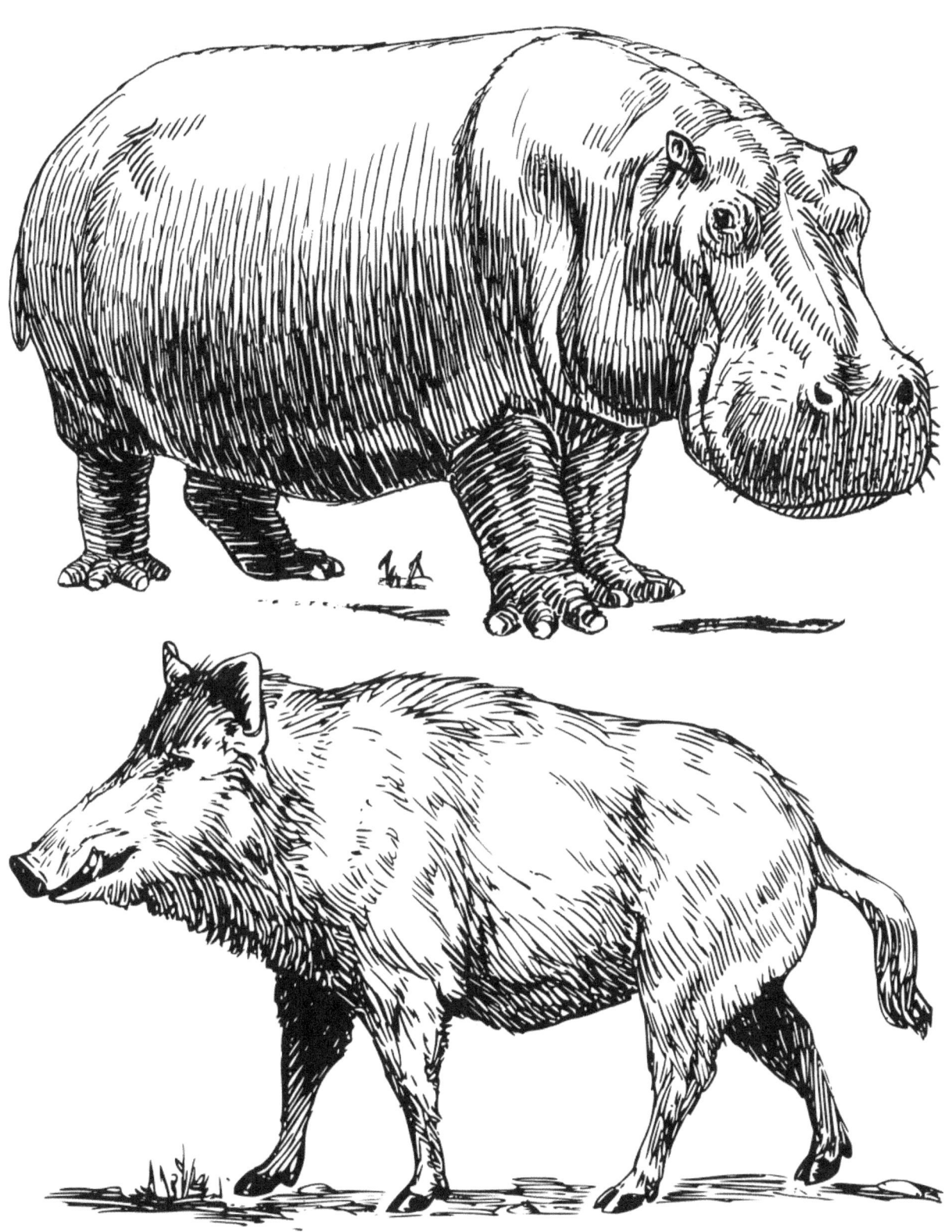

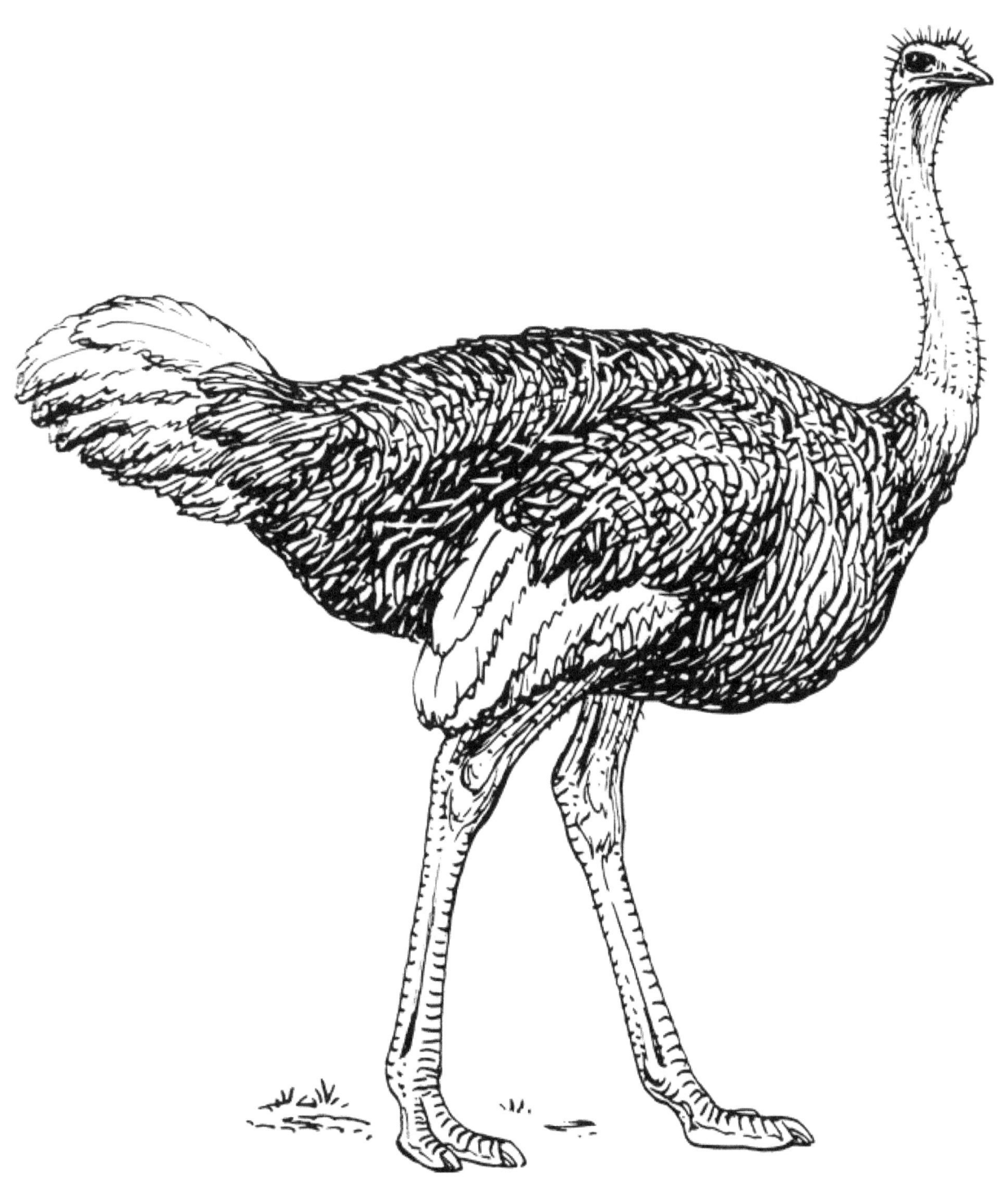

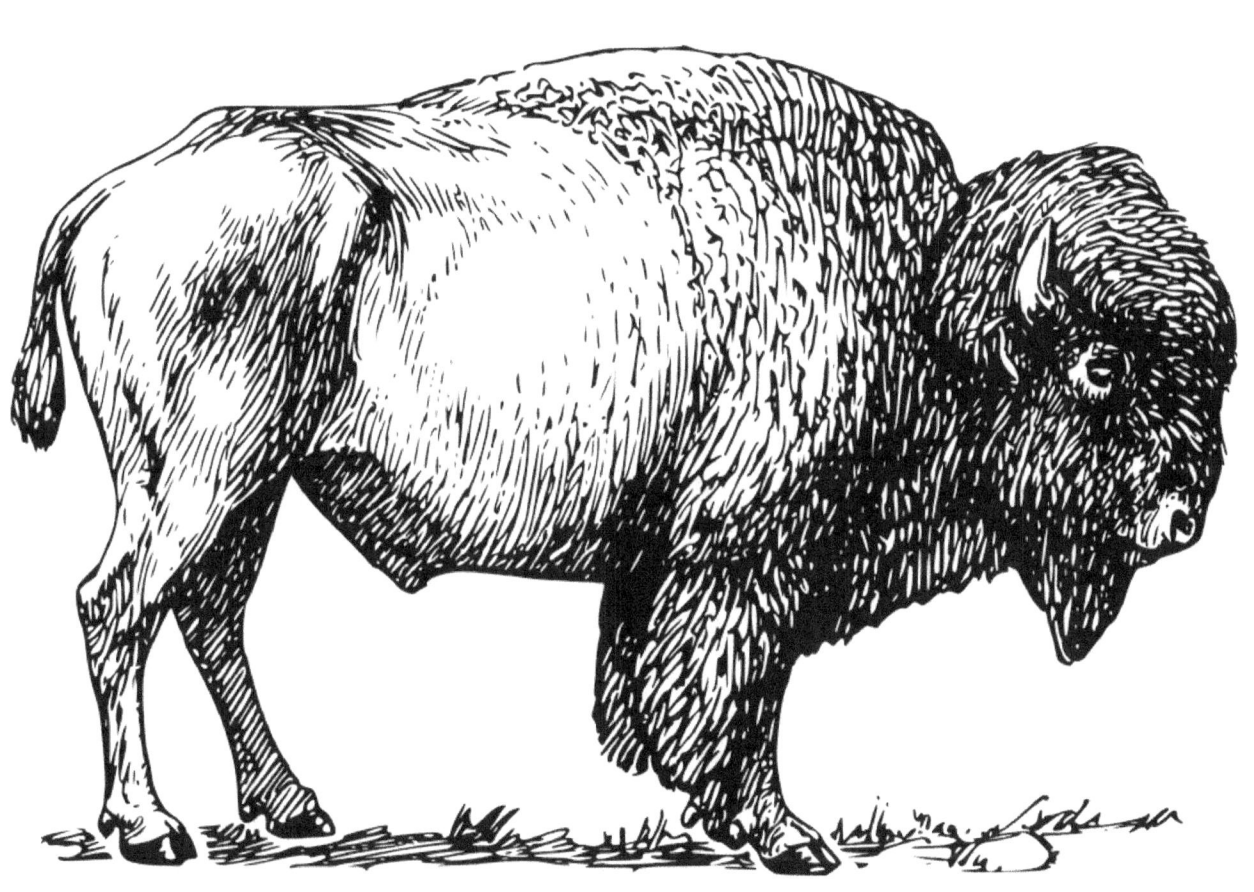

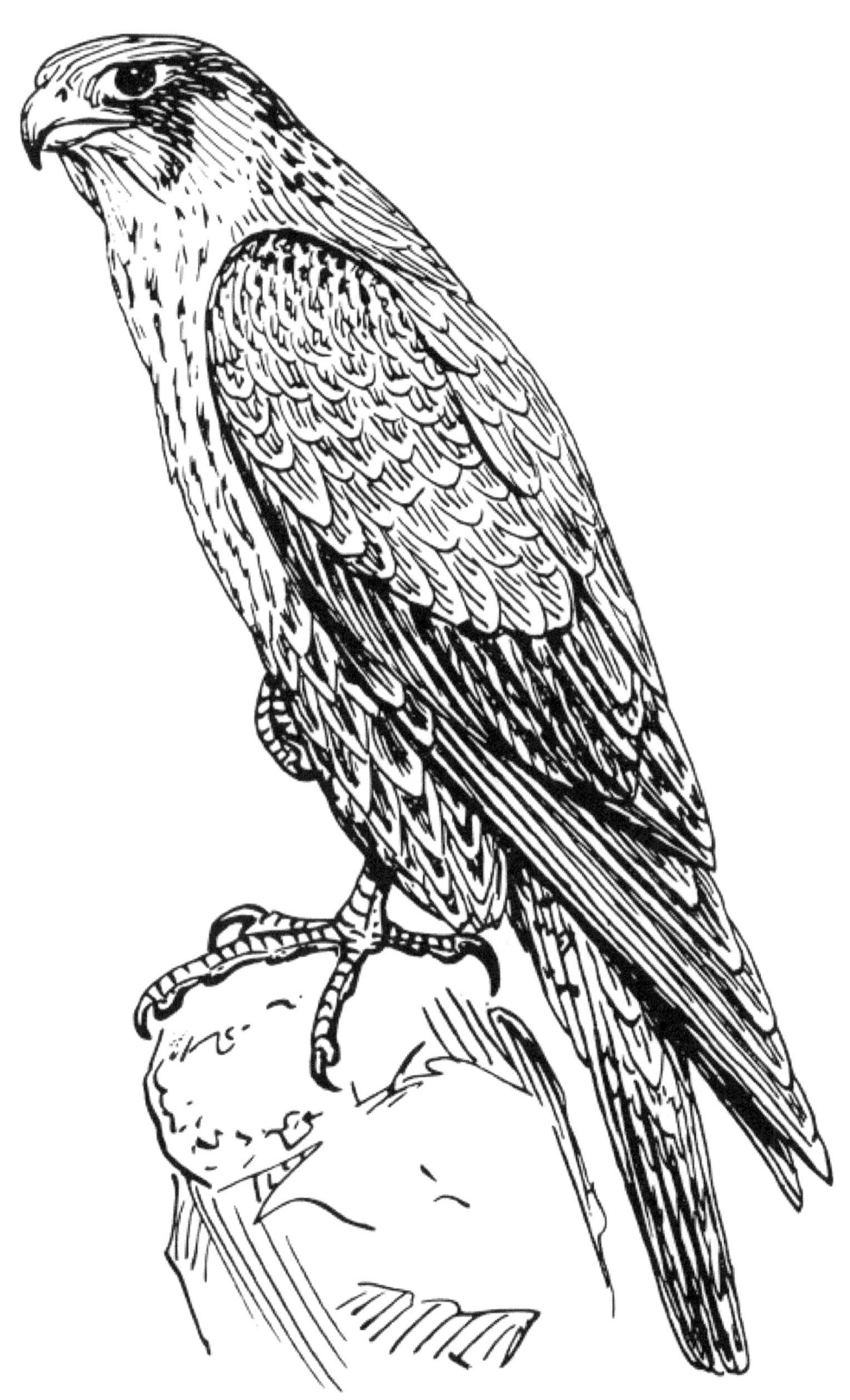

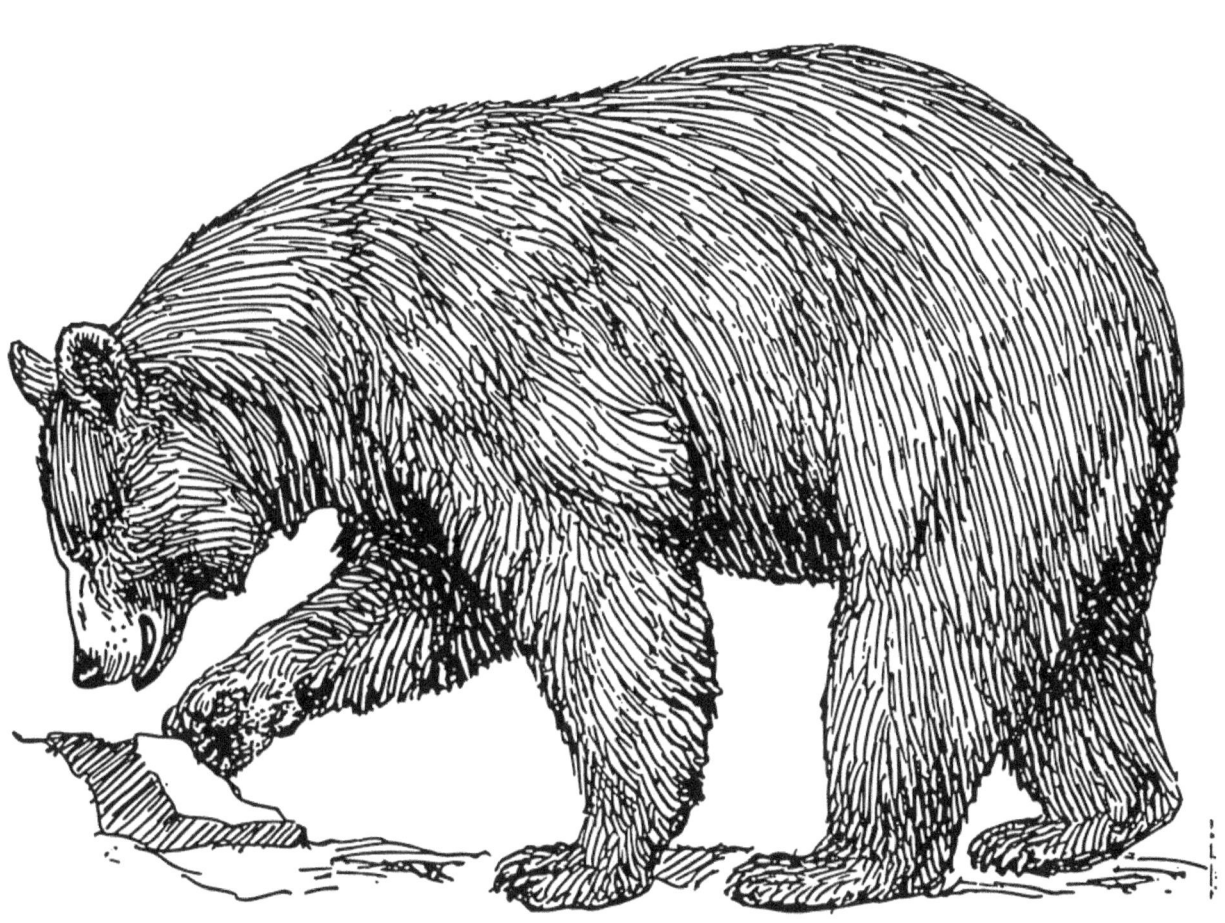

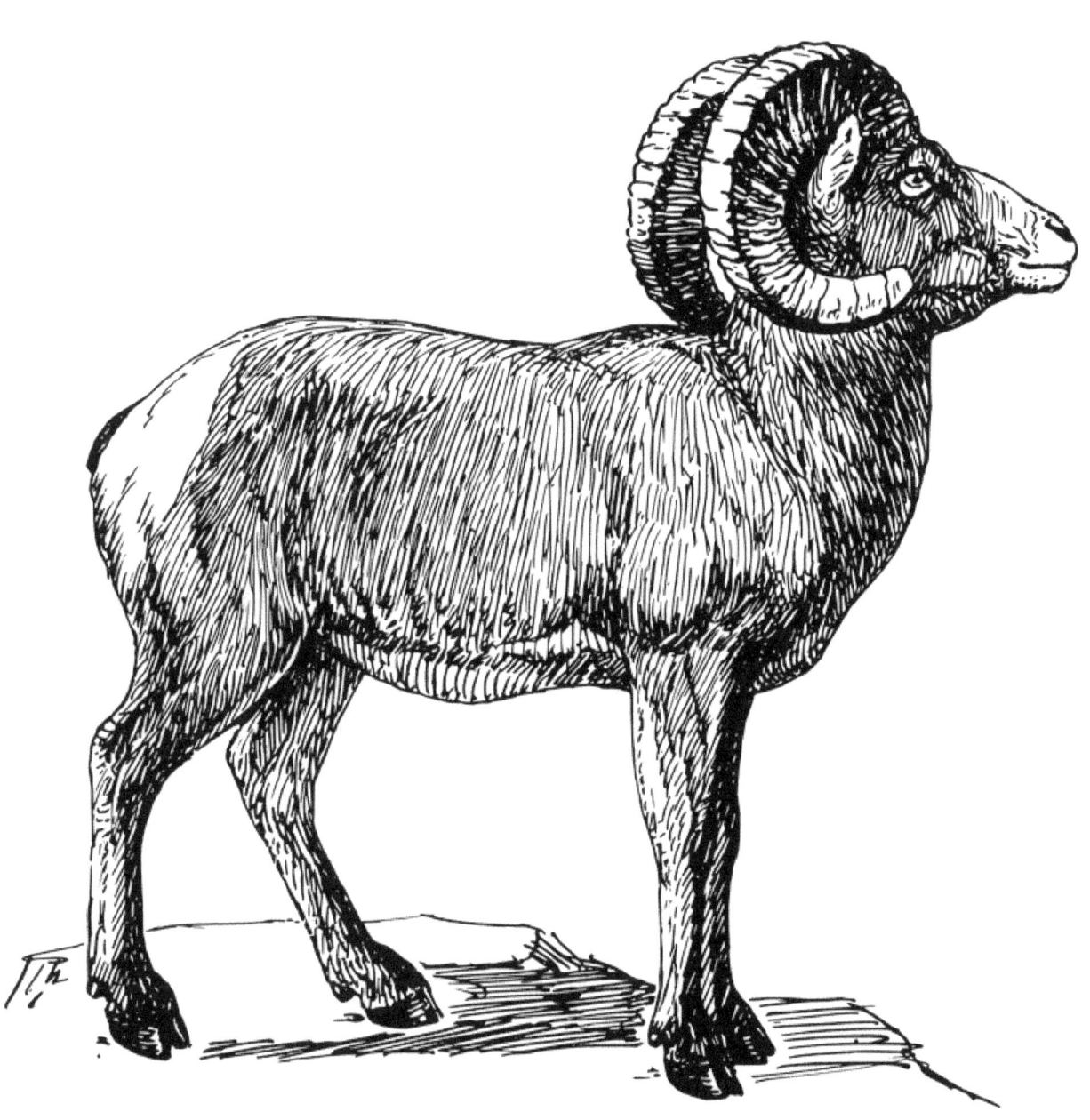

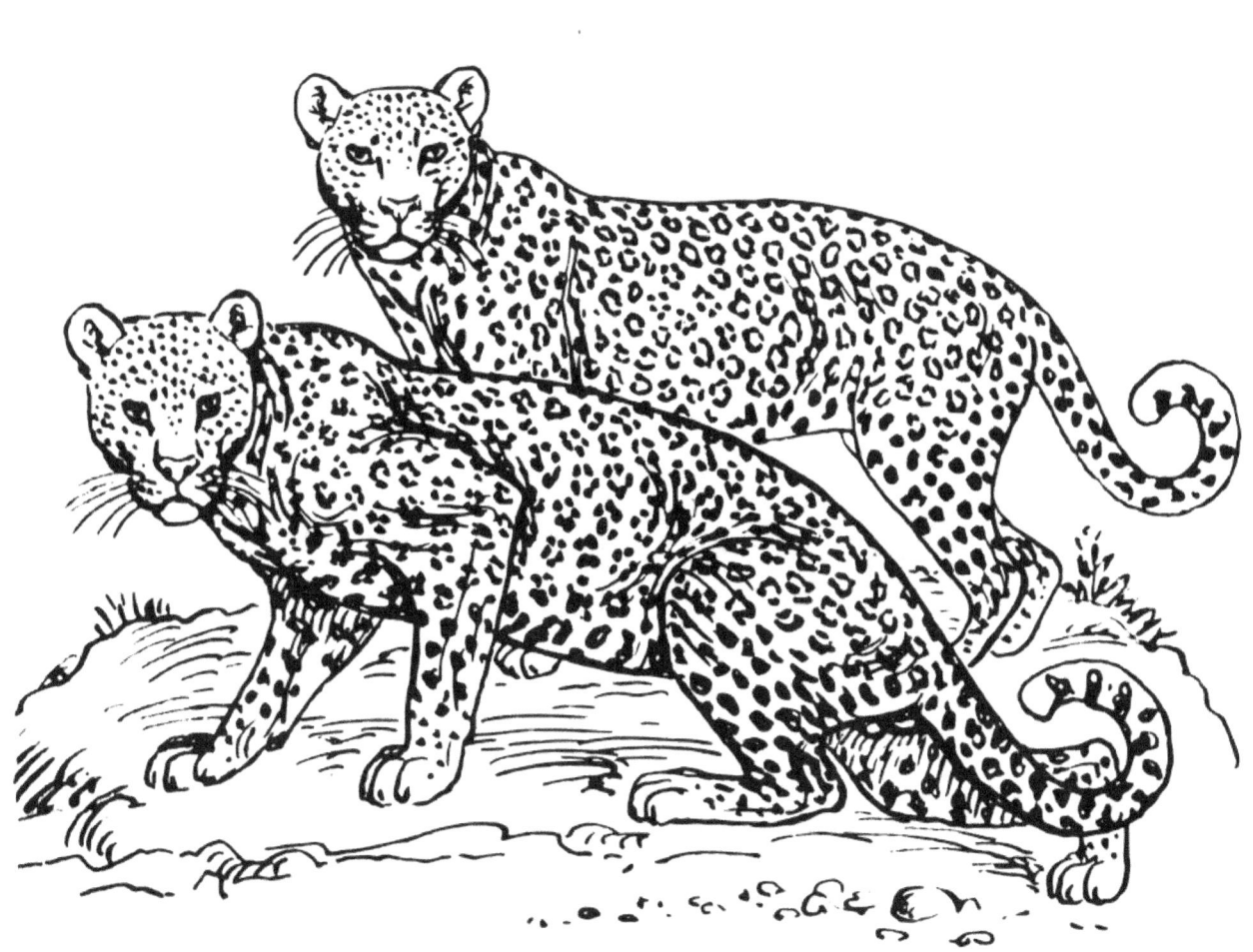

Enjoy even more *Colouring Books for Grown-Ups,* including:

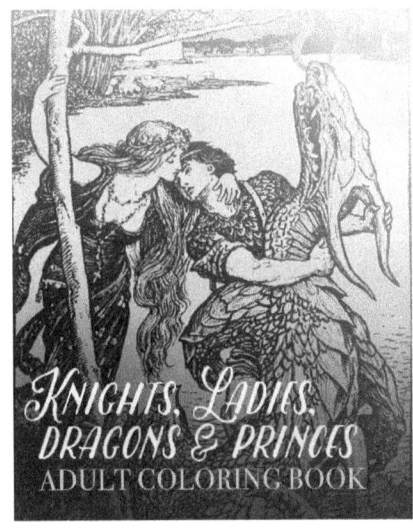
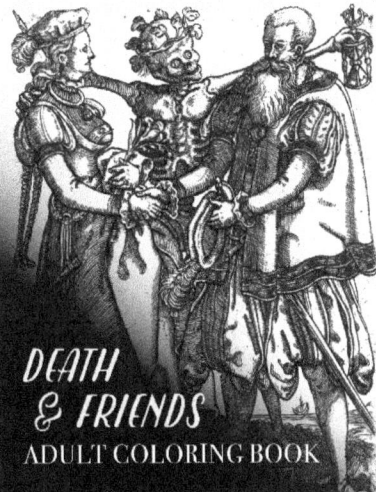
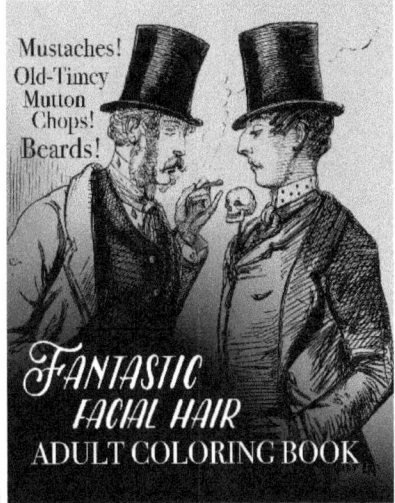
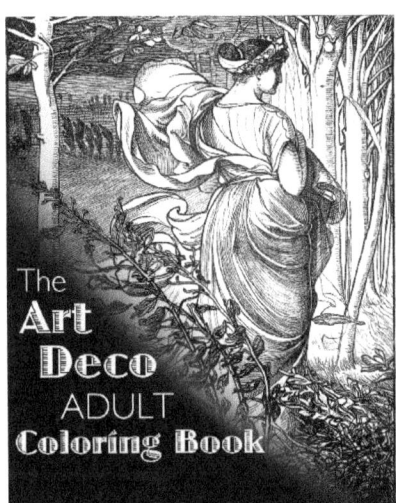
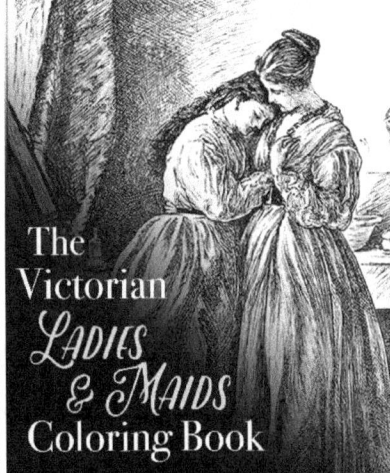
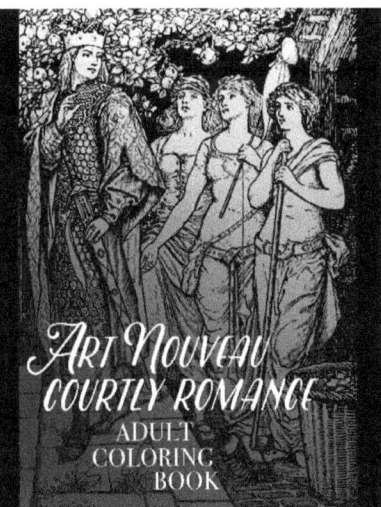

www.ingramcontent.com/pod-product-compliance
Lightning Source LLC
Chambersburg PA
CBHW080441220526
45465CB00007B/2723